HELP! I POO MY
British Edition

7 year old Toby is a problem using t... other people's homes, or in the boys toilets at school or in public toilets, so he tries to keep his poo inside himself instead. He also does this at home when he doesn't want to stop playing and refuses to listen to his body.

Because he tries to avoid going to the toilet, Toby often poos his pants, which he finds really embarrassing. He also wets himself sometimes when his poo pushes on his bladder. At school he wears pull-ups and his Mum has to come in to change him when he soils himself in the classroom. And he nearly always needs changing on days out, which makes him feel like he is a toddler.

Can his Mum and Dad, his big sister, his best friend and his new babysitter persuade Toby to use the toilet every time he needs to poo? Can he find the courage to poo in the school toilets? Or will he always have accidents in his pants and be known by his classmates as the Stinky Kid?

Also available:
HELP! I POO MY PANTS – FOR GIRLS

For children aged 8 to 12
who soil their pants:
A BOY LIKE YOU
A GIRL LIKE YOU

HELP! I POO MY PANTS For Boys
British Edition

James Parkin

www.bigredsock.com

First published 2020

Copyright © James Parkin 2020

The right of James Parkin to be identified as the Author of this Work has been asserted by him in accordance with the Copyright, Designs and Patents Act 1988.

All rights reserved. No part of this publication may be reproduced, stored in a retrieval system, or transmitted in any form or by any means electronic, mechanical, photocopying, recording or otherwise, without the prior permission of the copyright owner.

All characters in this publication are fictitious and any resemblance to real persons, living or dead, is purely coincidental.

Images on the covers and inside pages of this book are copyright and used under licence. All photographs are posed by models.

ACKNOWLEDGEMENTS

A big thank you to all the parents who have commented on my books for children who soil, saying that they had helped them to understand more about the condition and begin a conversation with their son or daughter about their soiling problems, and particularly to those who told me that my books had encouraged their child to try to poo on the toilet.

Many thanks to the wonderful staff and volunteers at ERIC for their support for this project, and for all they do to help children and their families deal with continence issues.

Grateful thanks to Valerie Duncan and Jaime Bruder for their assistance with the American Edition of this book.

Thank you to my friend Dimity Telfer for encouraging me to write more widely about my childhood soiling, and for her own efforts to spread awareness of encopresis.

A big thank you to my wonderful mother, not least for all the times during my childhood when she cleaned me up after I had pooed myself. Sorry for all the dirty pants, Mum!

AND…

To every child who has refused to tease another kid who has wee'd or pooed their pants…

To every parent who has done everything they can think of to help their child overcome their soiling problems…

To every adult who has consoled and helped someone else's child who has toilet issues…

To every member of the medical profession who helps children and young people to overcome continence issues…

To every member of nursery and school staff who has changed children who are past potty training age after they have wet or soiled themselves…

THANK YOU

CONTENTS

1	Accident in the Car	9
2	Hide and Seek	14
3	The Mean Babysitter	17
4	Talking with Mum	21
5	Pooing is Not the Same as Weeing	28
6	You Can't Make Poo Disappear	33
7	The Stinky Kid	37
8	I Really Need to Poo	41
9	What a Mess!	45
10	A Chat with Big Sister	49
11	Getting in Sarah's Car with Dirty Pants	53
12	Surviving the Sniff Test	56
13	Tummy Ache	62
14	Oh No!	64
15	Be Brave, Toby	67
16	The Biggest, Smelliest Poo in the World	71
17	A Dirty Pull-Up and a Happy Mum	76
18	The New Babysitter	80
19	A Toilet Sit and an Idea	84
20	A Poo at the Museum	88
21	Meeting a Girl who Pooed her Pants	94
22	Can I do a Poo in the School Toilets?	99
23	The Happiest Boy in the School	105
24	No More Stinky Kid!	107
25	I'm Proud of my Poos!	110
	Message by Torchlight	114
	About the Author	120
	Facebook	123
	ERIC – The Children's Bowel and Bladder Charity	128

Chapter 1
ACCIDENT IN THE CAR

'Toby's pooed his pants again,' calls out Louisa. She's my big sister and she's sitting next to me on the back seat of the car.

I've been sitting in poo for at least five miles. Louisa has guessed that it's more than just farts that she can smell. She usually knows when my pants are dirty.

Mum is sitting in the front seat, next to Dad who is driving. I hear her sigh. 'Oh Toby, that's the second time today. You had an accident at the Adventure Playground this morning.'

'Sorry, Mum,' I say.

'Toby, I asked you if you wanted to go to the toilet before we left Uncle Roger's house,' says Dad, 'and you said you didn't.'

'Sorry, Dad,' I say. I'd known that I needed the toilet before we'd got into the car. But I've never been able to poo at other people's houses. And I wasn't going to use the toilets at the Adventure Playground this morning, no way!

'I'm getting really fed up of this,' Dad says. He's talking to Mum, but I can still hear him. 'He's 7 years old and he still messes his pants. Is he ever going to grow out of it?'

'Well, you know he has problems using the toilet,' says Mum. 'He doesn't mess himself on purpose. We'd better look for somewhere to change him. I don't like to leave him sitting in his poo.'

No, I think, don't do that. Take me home. Change me there.

'Do we have to?' asks Dad. 'If he's not too messy then maybe we can leave it until we get home. It's not like he's running around and making the mess worse. You know I planned to watch the match on TV this evening. I don't want to miss the kick-off.'

Yes! Thanks, Dad!

Mum doesn't say anything for a minute. I'm hoping that means she agrees with Dad. But then the nasty smell coming from my pants and my bottom reaches her nose. 'Oh, I can smell him from here. It's no good, he's going to stink up the whole car. And it's not fair on Louisa. She's sitting right next to him, don't forget. She shouldn't have to smell her brother's poo for the next hour.'

'I don't mind,' says Louisa.

She does mind, I'm sure she does. I can feel the poo in my pants, but I can't really smell it myself. But I know that I stink to other people. And nobody wants to sit next to a pooey kid. Louisa is just being nice to me. She knows that I don't like having my pants changed in public toilets.

'Look,' says Mum, pointing to a sign on the side of the road, 'there's a shopping centre ahead. I can clean him up there.'

Oh no! I hate being changed in shopping centres. Now I'll have to walk to the toilets with Mum, who will be carrying my telltale changing bag. It's a Saturday, so they'll be hundreds of adults and kids around. Everyone who comes near me will smell what I've done. Loads of people will know that I've pooed myself.

When we reach the toilets Mum will take off my trousers and pants. And then I'll have to stand there, holding up my jumper, while she cleans my bum with baby wipes. It makes me feel like I'm about 3 years old.

Or she'll take me into a baby changing

room where I'll have to stand bare bummed, being cleaned up alongside babies and toddlers. And I'll be hoping that no little kids come in and stare at me while their parents are changing their baby brothers and sisters.

If my pants are really messy, Mum will throw them away. Even if they're one of my favourite pairs. I'm sorry Toby, she'll say, but I'm not carrying pooey pants around with me. If you want to keep them, then keep them clean. This morning I watched my *Horrid Henry* pants being bagged up and thrown in the bin at the Adventure Playground.

I watch miserably as we turn off the motorway towards the shopping centre.

I hate having dirty pants.

I hate having
dirty pants

Chapter 2
HIDE AND SEEK

Another Saturday. My best friend Oliver has come round to play at my house.

Okay, Oliver is my only real friend. It's hard to keep friends when you have accidents on playdates. But Oliver doesn't mind. He's been my friend since we were at playgroup together. And I've only stank up his bedroom once.

Right now we're playing Hide and Seek in my garden. I'm hiding and he's seeking. I've got a really good hiding place between the shed and the fence. I don't think Oliver knows it exists. He'll never find me.

Oh no, not now! Why does my body always tell me to poo at the wrong times? I can't leave my hiding place. Oliver will see me and then I'll lose the game. Rotten body! I went for a wee just before we started playing. Why couldn't you have told me to do a poo then?

Only one thing for it. I'll have to hold it in. Make the feeling go away. Then I'll go to the toilet after we've finished the game. Or maybe when Oliver has gone home. Don't worry, I've done this lots of times, I know what to do.

I stand up straight against the back of the shed. I cross my legs and breathe in, pulling my poo back into my body instead of pushing it out of my bum.

The feeling hasn't gone away. I cross my legs tighter and try harder. My face is screwed up as I fight my body. This is really hard this time. When did I last use the toilet? Did I do a poo yesterday? No, I didn't. The day before? Don't think so. The day before the day before? Not sure.

Phew, done it! The feeling has gone away at last. Ha, take that, body! That will teach you not to tell me to poo in the middle of a game. Don't worry, it'll remind me later to go to the toilet. I'll go then for sure.

Okay, back to Hide and Seek. I can hear Oliver calling that's he's coming to get me. Oh no you're not, Oliver, you'll never find me!

Germs love unwashed hands!

Chapter 3
THE MEAN BABYSITTER

Oliver went home after we'd finished playing Hide and Seek. Now Mum and Dad have gone out. Tina is babysitting me and Louisa. I'm playing Snakes and Ladders with Tina, while Louisa is reading a book.

And then it happens. I have an accident. It's the poo that I'd held back while I was playing with Oliver. It comes out of my bum and goes in my pants while I'm sitting on the floor of the lounge. Right in the middle of the game of Snakes and Ladders.

I don't say anything about it to Tina. She was really cross with me the last time she'd had to change me. I carry on playing and ignore the fact that my pants are dirty.

Of course, Tina soon finds out. 'What's that smell? Toby, you'd better not have pooed your pants again.'

I say nothing. I know what's coming next.

'Stand up and turn around,' orders Tina.

I do what she says. My bottom is now facing her.

Tina pulls down my trousers and looks in my pants. I wish she wouldn't do this in front of Louisa. 'Oh you have, you dirty little boy. I can't believe you've done this again. Messy pants, at your age. And the last time I looked after you, you wet yourself as well. You're such a baby.'

Yes, now and again I also wet my pants. I really can't help doing that.

Tina goes on, 'You should be wearing a nappy, not big boy pants. Didn't your parents potty train you at all? Or are you just too lazy to go to the toilet?'

'No, I'm not,' I reply. I'm telling the truth. I'm not too lazy to use the toilet. It's just that my body tells me to poo at the wrong time. Or it doesn't tell me at all. Like tonight. Why didn't my body remind me to go for a poo?

Tina is not impressed. 'Well, you could have fooled me. Next time I babysit you I'm going to bring some nappies with me. You definitely need them.'

I start to cry. I can't help it. I already feel bad about pooing my pants in front of a babysitter. And that she's going to be changing me like a toddler again soon. Why does Tina have to be so horrible to me?

'That's it, cry like a baby as well,' she says. 'Perhaps I'd better bring a dummy with me as well. Tell me why I shouldn't treat you like a baby when you act like one.'

I can't answer her. I try, but I can't. It's really hard to talk when you're crying.

'Don't be so mean to him,' says Louisa. 'Mum's told you that he has toilet problems. He can't help it.'

'Well, that's strange,' says Tina, 'seeing that every other 7 year old boy manages to keep his pants clean.'

'That's not true', says Louisa. 'Loads of kids his age still poo their pants. Mum showed me a website all about it. It's called "Soiling". And lots of kids who are much older than Toby still do it. Even some teenagers do. It's a lot more common than you think and…'

'Louisa!' snaps Tina. 'Would you like to help me to clean your darling brother's pooey bottom? No? Well, if you don't want to clean up his poo, like I've got to do, then I suggest that you go back to reading your book and be quiet. When I want advice on childcare from a 10 year old girl, I'll ask for

19

it.'

Louisa goes back to reading her book and doesn't say anything else about my toilet problems. But she is right. I used to think that I was the only kid my age in the whole world who still pooed his pants. But now I know I'm not. Lots of boys and girls have the same problem as me.

Tina stands up and grabs my arm. 'Come on, you big baby, let's go and change your pants.' She pushes me towards the stairs. 'Get yourself up to the bathroom and start getting undressed. Leave your pants on until I'm ready to remove them, I don't want you getting poo all over the bathroom floor. And you can forget about finishing that game. Or watching Netflix. As soon as I've cleaned up your mess, you're going straight to bed.'

Chapter 4
TALKING WITH MUM

I'm still awake when Mum comes home and walks into my bedroom. I've stopped crying, but my pillow is still damp from my tears. Tina carried on telling me off the whole time she was changing my pants. Then she put me straight to bed, like she had said she would. No bedtime story. No goodnight kiss.

'Hello, my precious,' Mum says as she sits on my bed. 'Come on, let's have a cuddle.'

I sit up and we hug. Mum holds me close for a long time. I start to feel a little bit better.

'Oh, my darling son,' says Mum, 'I'm so sorry about what happened to you tonight.'

'Tina was horrible to me,' I say, still with my arms wrapped tightly around Mum. 'She says she's going to bring nappies and a dummy next time she babysits me. And when Louisa tried to stick up for me, she was nasty to her too.'

'I know, Louisa has told me all about it.' Mum finally lets me go and I sit up in my bed. 'Don't worry, Toby, Tina will never be looking after you again. I've given her the sack.'

I don't understand what she means. 'The sack?'

Mum smiles. 'It means that she's not your babysitter anymore. I'll find someone else to look after you and Louisa.'

I lean forward to hug her again. 'Thank you, thank you. I really didn't like it when Tina was so mean to me. I love you, Mum.'

'I love you too, my precious,' she says as she hugs me back. 'And nobody upsets my little boy and gets away with it. I had some pretty sharp words for young Tina. I think she was almost crying by the time I'd finished.'

Mum lets me go from this second hug. I feel much happier as I lean back against the headboard of my bed. 'Can I have a nice babysitter like Charlie again?' I ask. He was my babysitter when I was 5. He never got cross with me when I had dirty pants or wet myself. He was always smiling, even when he was cleaning poo off my bum. And he gave me lots of cuddles. I really liked him.

'Of course I'll try to get you a nice babysitter,' says Mum. 'And it may not be such a bad thing that you gave Charlie such a lot of practice at cleaning your bottom! He works with 3 and 4 year olds at a day nursery now. And his mother tells me that he deals with most of the toilet accidents that happen there. Nearly all the kids go to him if they wee or poo themselves.'

I could guess why! I knew that Charlie wouldn't tell off any little kid who forgot to go to the toilet. And, thanks to me, he was great with dealing with wet legs and pooey bums!

Then Mum speaks in a more serious voice. 'But Toby, you're older now, and you sometimes make quite a big mess in your pants. And cleaning up a pooey 7 year old is a pretty nasty job, especially when it's not your kid. Your Dad and I are used to changing your pants, but it can come as a bit of a shock to anyone else. Do you understand that?'

I nod. It's not very nice for me either. I really don't like it when I have to be changed by a babysitter, or a friend's mum, or an aunt or uncle. Not that any aunts or uncles are willing to look after me and change me these days. 'He can stay here without you when he's fully toilet trained,' Auntie Fiona had told my Mum. 'As he isn't, you'll have to stay with him if you want him to come to Robin's birthday party.'

Mum goes on, 'If you could try a little harder to use the toilet, then that really would make life easier for everyone. That special medicine I give you every day makes your poo nice and soft. It doesn't hurt when you go to the toilet anymore, does it?'

'No,' I say.

'So will you try to go a bit more often?'

'I'll try.'

'Good boy. Now, do you know when you last did a poo in the toilet?'

I shake my head. 'I can't remember.'

'Okay. Well, do you know the last time you needed to poo and held it in?'

This time I nod my head. 'It was when I was playing Hide and Seek in the garden with Oliver. I was hiding behind the shed when I felt it.'

'That was this afternoon, wasn't it?'

I nod again.

'Right,' says Mum, 'so you could have stopped playing the game for a few minutes to go to the toilet, couldn't you?'

'I suppose so,' I reply. 'But I had a really good hiding place. I didn't want to lose it.'

'And was keeping your hiding place worth all the upset you had tonight?' asks Mum.

'No,' I say. Mum is right. It really wasn't worth it.

Do you need to poo?

"I didn't go to the toilet and now I've pooed my pants."

"I couldn't hold it in any longer."

**Don't try to hold it in!
It wants to come out!**

What should you do?

> I didn't go to the toilet and now I've wet my pants.

> The poo I held inside my body pressed on my bladder and made me wee myself.

Go to the toilet!
Let it go!

Chapter 5
POOING IS NOT THE SAME AS WEEING

'But I was going to go to the toilet after Oliver had gone home,' I say to Mum. She is still sitting on my bed. 'I really was. But my body didn't remind me to poo. Not once. It just made me do it in my pants. In front of Tina and Louisa. Why didn't it remind me? And why does it keep telling me to poo at the wrong times? Like when I'm playing a game? Or when I'm at school? Or round someone's house or at the park? It's not fair.'

'Oh, Toby,' Mum says, 'you can't always expect your body to tell you to poo when you want it to. You may need to poo at any time, wherever you are or whatever you're doing. And that's when you should go to the toilet. Sometimes I need to poo when I'm at work. So I have to stop what I'm doing to use the staff toilets. And I don't care if anyone else knows what I'm doing. Everyone poos, remember?'

I nod. Mum and Dad have told me this lots of times.

Mum goes on, 'As for your body not reminding you, well…what happens when you feel you need to wee?'

'I don't always feel I have to wee,' I remind her. 'Sometimes I don't know I need to wee until I start doing it and wet my pants.'

'I know, love,' says Mum, 'that's when you have a big poo stuck inside you and it pushes on your bladder. Then you just wee, wherever you are. But normally what happens when you need a wee? If you don't go to the toilet, then the feeling just gets stronger, doesn't it?'

I nod.

'And if you keep ignoring the feeling, then it gets stronger and stronger. That's your body's way of telling you that you really must go to the toilet soon or you'll have an accident. Eventually it gets so bad that it may hurt a bit and you find it hard to stand still.'

'And you might start fidgeting,' I add. I

was remembering what happened at school in an assembly last year. I was sitting next to a girl in my class called Lucy. After a while she couldn't seem to sit still and she began fidgeting a lot. Then she wet her pants and made a huge puddle on the floor. I had to jump up and move out of the way of her wee.

'Yes,' agrees Mum. 'In the end it can become so bad that you'll either have to find somewhere, anywhere, to wee or you'll wet your pants. Do you remember when you were 4 and you were at Auntie Fiona's house? You became desperate for a wee while your aunt was in the bathroom with your cousin Jessica.'

I do remember. 'I was 4 and a bit,' I say, 'and I was really bursting.' Jessica had just stopped wearing nappies and she was taking ages using the toilet. I knew that I couldn't hold it any longer. 'I'm gonna wee my pants,' I said miserably.

Louisa came to my rescue. She grabbed the biscuit barrel off the table and dumped the biscuits onto the floor. I just stood there watching her, not knowing what she was doing. But then she yanked down my trousers and pants and held the biscuit barrel in place while I stood there and used it as a potty.

Auntie Fiona and Jessica came back just as I'd finished weeing. Louisa was pleased with herself for her quick thinking, and she knew that Mum and Dad would be pleased with her for helping her little brother. I was grateful to her and pleased that I had avoided wetting my pants. Auntie Fiona wasn't pleased with either of us! She was cross that I'd gone to the toilet in her lounge and destroyed her biscuit barrel. But at least I hadn't made a wet patch on her carpet. Or wee'd all over the custard creams!

'Anyway,' says Mum, 'pooing is not the same as weeing. If your body tells you to poo and you ignore it and hold it in, your body may not tell you again. It may just decide to push the poo into your pants, wherever you are. That's why you have to go to the toilet when you need to. You may not get a reminder.'

Please don't wee in any biscuit barrels! I only did it because I really, really had to go! And try not to use your Mum's favourite vase as a toilet, like this little boy and girl have!

Chapter 6
YOU CAN'T MAKE POO DISAPPEAR

'But why does my body do that?' I ask. 'Why does it make me have an accident at the park? Or in a shop? Or at school? It must know that I hate it when I poo myself in those places.'

'Well, Toby,' replies Mum, 'you know that you can't make poo disappear. Holding it in only gets rid of the feeling, not the poo itself. You know that, don't you?'

I nod. When I was younger I used to think I had made my poo disappear by making the feeling that I needed the toilet go away. At the time I couldn't understand how I kept having accidents and my poo kept ending up in my pants.

'So,' Mum goes on, 'your poo has to go somewhere. And if it doesn't go in the toilet then it has to go somewhere else. When you were a baby and you were too young to use the potty or the toilet, your poo had to go in your nappy. Now if you don't use the toilet, your poo has to go in your pants. Or in your pyjama bottoms. Or in your pull-up at school.'

Okay, I have to wear pull-ups when I'm at school. Mrs Mattock, my teacher, insists that I do. She told Mum that I couldn't wear normal pants if I kept wetting and soiling myself in the classroom. Yes, I've had a lot of accidents at school.

Actually, I don't mind wearing pull-ups too much. At least I don't leave a puddle on my chair if I wet myself. Or on the classroom floor. And no, I don't wee in my pull-up on purpose if I don't feel like going to the toilet. Well, not often.

Mum carries on, 'So you see, Toby, your body just wants to get rid of the poo. Keeping poo inside you is not good for you. It's not healthy. It can make you really poorly. So your body has to push it out. It gives you the chance to go to the toilet. It knows you don't want to be messy and smelly. But if you ignore it, then it has no choice. It makes you do it in your pants, wherever you are. Do you understand that?'

'Yes,' I say.

'Good. Because your body isn't your enemy. It wants to be your friend. It doesn't want you to have accidents. It wants you to poo in the toilet. You just have to listen to your body, instead of fighting it. Listen to what it's telling you. And then act on it. Okay, I think we've got just enough time for a bedtime story before you go to sleep.'

'And a goodnight kiss?' I ask

'Of course, my precious.'

Can't do a poo? Toot on the loo!

I'm finding it hard to push my poo out of my bum.

Try playing a toy trumpet while you're sitting on the toilet.

He's not joking! We use the same muscles for blowing that we use for pooing!

Running around is also good for getting poo moving. And boys can try sitting down on the toilet to do a wee sometimes. There could also be a poo ready to come out!

Chapter 7
THE STINKY KID

I walk into my classroom on Monday morning. The first thing I see is Rachit and Leo looking at party invitations. I hear Leo say, 'I think Freddie has invited every boy in the class to his birthday party.'

Then Rachit sees me and says, 'Except for the Stinky Kid, of course. Freddie doesn't want a party pooper there!' Both boys start laughing.

I ignore them and walk over to my table. I haven't been to a birthday party for ages. I tell myself that I don't care. I don't want to go to Freddie's stupid party anyway.

Oliver always invites me to his party, of course. But his birthday isn't for months and months. Since he moved house, he now goes to a different school to me. It's sad that he now lives six miles away, so I don't see him after school either. But at least we still have playdates on Saturdays when we can.

Nearly everyone in my class calls me the Stinky Kid. Isaac started it and everyone copied him. They all know that I'm wearing a pull-up because they can see it when we change for PE. For a while they called me Nappy Boy, but these days I'm the Stinky Kid.

I hope that I don't need to poo while I'm at school today. If I do I'll just have to cross my legs under the table and breathe in. Hopefully I can keep it in until I get home. Usually I can, but sometimes I can't.

Accidents at school are the worst. Another kid quickly smells when I've got a dirty pull-up and tells Mrs Mattock. I dread it when I see someone's hand go up after I've had an accident. Are they just going to ask a question, or are they going to say, 'Toby smells,' or, 'Toby stinks,' or, 'Toby's pooed his pull-up,' to my teacher? Then half the class will hold their noses and Mrs Mattock will make me walk over to her. If she agrees that I smell pooey, she'll tell me to go to the Office to see the School Secretary.

When I get there Mrs Greenwood will call my Mum. 'I'm afraid Toby has messed his pull-up again,' she'll say, 'can you come in and change him, please.'

Then I'll have to sit in my dirty pull-up on a chair in the corridor. Mrs Greenwood doesn't want me stinking up her office. It takes Mum about 20 minutes to get to my school, but it seems like hours while I'm waiting.

Last time two older girls walked past me. 'Phew!' said the first girl, 'that boy stinks.'

The other girl said, 'He's in my little sister's class. He wears pull-ups and he's always pooing in them. They call him the Stinky Kid.'

The two girls went off laughing. Great! Did the whole school know me as the Stinky Kid now?

Mum is fed up of having to come into school to change my pull-up. She doesn't say so, but I know she is. I heard her saying to Dad once that her boss at work isn't happy about it either. I don't know why. Her boss doesn't come to my school and change me, thank goodness!

I'm really fed up of it as well. But what can I do? Go to the boys toilets? No way! I have never, ever, pooed in the school toilets and I never, ever will. I would rather kiss Matilda, who's always picking her nose and eating her bogeys, than do that.

Please body, don't tell me to do a poo at school today. Or if you do, let me hold it in until I go home. Please don't make me have another accident. Please!

Chapter 8
I REALLY NEED TO POO

It's Saturday again. Another playdate with Oliver, this time at his house. It's raining, so we're having to play indoors. We spent ages in his bedroom, playing board games and playing with his *Star Wars* figures and playing on his tablet. I needed to poo at one point, but I held it in. I've been to the toilet to do a wee since I got here. Oliver's done two wees! But I'm not going to do a poo at Oliver's house, of course. It's okay, the feeling went away, so we carried on playing.

At half past twelve Oliver's Mum gave us lunch. It was yummy. Now we're sitting downstairs, watching TV. I'm really enjoying the programme, when the feeling comes back again. It's much worse this time. I try to hold it in while I'm sitting there, but it's no good. My poo wants to come out. No, not now!

I stand up and grip the side of the sofa. I

cross my legs really tightly and screw my face up. This is really starting to hurt. I cross my legs even tighter, as tight as I possibly can. My body is not going to beat me. I'm going to keep this poo inside me, I am, I am, I am!

'Mum,' calls out Oliver, 'I think Toby is feeling sick.'

Seconds later Oliver's Mum rushes into the room. She is carrying a washing-up bowl. She looks at me, holding onto the sofa like I'm about to fall over. She looks at my crossed legs and my screwed-up face. She guesses what I'm doing. 'Toby, do you need to go to the toilet?' she asks.

'No,' I lie.

She doesn't believe me. 'Tell me the truth, Toby. Do you need to do a poo?'

'No!' Well, what do you expect me to say? Yes, I badly need to do a poo, but I can't use the toilet at your house, so I'm desperately trying not to do it in my pants. I don't think so!

The feeling finally goes away. Phew! I uncross my legs and sit down on the sofa again. 'I'm okay,' I say. I look at the washing-up bowl. 'I'm not going to barf.'

'No,' says Oliver's Mum, 'I think the

problem is at the other end. I'm not going to try to force you to use the toilet, Toby. You're old enough to decide for yourself when you need to go. But I hope you're not going to mess your pants again. I'll be disappointed if I have to change you because you've had another accident.' She goes back into the kitchen, taking the washing-up bowl with her.

I go back to watching TV with Oliver. His mum has changed me a few times when I've had an accident at her house. She doesn't want to send me home early, but she really doesn't like having to clean me up. I can tell that she's trying not to look disgusted when she sees what I've done in my pants. At least she doesn't make me wear a pull-up when I visit, like Auntie Fiona now does.

It'll be okay this time, I decide. Dad is going to be picking me up again soon. I'll use the toilet as soon as we get home. I'm not going to have an accident.

Somewhere new? Use the loo!

> Being willing to use any toilet is an important lifeskill.

> Try to use the loo when you go somewhere new!

> And you CAN poo at a friend's home! I just have!

You ARE allowed to go Number 2!

Chapter 9
WHAT A MESS!

'Oh Toby, what a mess!' says Dad as he pulls down my pants. I've already taken off all my other clothes, so he can change me. 'How long is it since you used the toilet?'

I shrug. I can't remember when I last did a poo. I look down and see my pants. Dad is right, they're really messy. He's having to be careful taking them off me. I can't see my bottom, of course, but it must be very messy as well.

As soon as I got back from Oliver's house, Louisa asked if I wanted to play on the Xbox with her. We played for ages and I totally forgot that I hadn't been to the toilet. Then I went up to my bedroom and played by myself for a while. And then it happened. I pooed my pants.

Dad sighs. 'Did you know you needed to poo while you were playing with Oliver?'

'Yes,' I say.

'Well, why didn't you go to the toilet there?'

'I can't,' I reply.

'Toby, it's just a toilet the same as the one you're standing right next to. It isn't going to bite your bum, y'know.'

I know it's not going to bite my bum. But I still can't sit on it.

Dad has finally got my pants off me. He drops them in the sink and turns the taps on. 'And did you carry on playing in your dirty pants after you'd pooed yourself? I think you must have done to have got them in that state.'

I nod. Dad's right. That's exactly what I did. I just carried on with my game, ignoring the fact that my pants were dirty. Afterwards I sat on my bed to read a book. Well, I wasn't going to go downstairs and tell Dad I'd pooed myself, was I?

He found out what I'd done when he came in to see if I wanted a drink. The smell in my bedroom told him straight away that I needed changing. The large brown patch on the seat of my trousers was another giveaway. So was the stain on my bedspread.

'Toby,' he says, 'you make the mess a lot worse when you play in dirty pants. Why on earth do you want to sit and stand and run around in your own poo? Don't you find it disgusting?'

I don't know what to say. I just stand there while Dad gets the worst of the mess off my bottom.

'And you know it's bad for you. Your Mum has told you that you could get an infection from sitting in poo. That will make it hurt when you do a wee.'

Yes, Mum did explain that to me. But I still can't tell anyone when I've had an accident. I carry on standing there in silence. I really don't like clean-up. And I really don't know how to answer Mum and Dad's questions about my poo problems.

'Okay, young man,' says Dad, 'let's get you in the shower and get the rest of this mess off of you. And afterwards you can sit on that toilet for ten minutes and see if there's any more to come out.'

Oh no! Ten minutes of total boredom.

Don't sit in your poo!

"Don't carry on wearing messy pants."

"Change yourself or tell someone that you've had an accident."

"Phew, he stinks! Remember, even if you can't smell your poo, other kids and adults can!"

Get changed!
Get clean!

Chapter 10
A CHAT WITH BIG SISTER

Sitting on the toilet was so boring. I had nothing to do. Dad wouldn't let me read or play a game on the tablet. He said I had to concentrate on pooing. But I couldn't do anything. I'd already done it all in my pants.

Happily I was able to get off after seven and a bit minutes. Louisa knocked on the bathroom door, saying she needed a wee. She could probably have waited, but I decided that she couldn't. I got off the toilet and escaped to my bedroom.

Now I'm sitting on my bed, reading a book. I hear the toilet flush. I'm not going back to sit on the toilet again, even if Louisa has finished her wee! I carry on reading.

Seconds later Louisa calls out at my bedroom door. 'Toby, can I come in?'

'Sure,' I reply, and I put down my book.

Louisa walks through the door and sits next to me on the bed. 'Wanted to see if you were okay,' she says. 'I couldn't help looking in the sink in the bathroom.'

Oh no, I forgot about that! She's seen my pooey pants. 'I had an accident,' I say in a quiet voice.

'A pretty bad one, huh? You really filled your pants this time, didn't you? My little brother can certainly make big messes!'

I nod. 'Dad wasn't very pleased about it. He guessed that I'd been playing in dirty pants for ages.'

'You never tell anyone when you're messy,' says Louisa. 'You always wait until someone smells it. Why do you do that? Mum and Dad don't usually tell you off for having accidents.'

Oh, I always find this question so hard to answer. I can never explain to grown-ups why I can't tell them when my pants are dirty. Maybe Louisa will understand if I tell her. 'It's just so…oh, what's that long word? Ember-something.'

'Embarrassing?' Louisa suggests.

'That's it. It's embarrassing. To have to tell someone that I've pooed myself at my age. I just can't do it. Remember last year when Lucy wet herself in assembly? I bet she felt really embarrassed about it.'

'That was that girl in your class, wasn't it?' asks Louisa.

I nod.

'Yes, I bet she did. She couldn't look at anyone while Miss Heggs was leading her out of the Hall. She kept her head down the whole time.'

'Exactly,' I say. 'Well, it's like that for me, except it's ten times worse, because I'm having accidents all the time.'

'But you know someone will find out sooner or later, don't you?'

'Yes,' I say. 'but I like to put it off as long as I can. Like when I used to hide my dirty pants at the back of the cupboard in my bedroom. I knew they'd be found one day. Especially when I started to run out of clean pants. But I thought at least Mum and Dad wouldn't find out I'd had an accident today. Or had another accident that day, if they'd already changed me once. I thought getting found out tomorrow, or next week, or next year, was better than today.'

'Mum was really angry when she discovered all the pants you'd hidden, wasn't she?' asks Louisa.

'Yes,' I reply. 'She made me promise to never, ever do it again. And I haven't. And I know they don't tell me off when I've had an accident. But I still feel like I've let Mum and Dad down. Even though they tell me I haven't let them down, I still feel that I have. I can't help it. I just hate the moment when I know that I've pooed myself and my pants are dirty. Hate it, hate it, hate it!'

Chapter 11
GETTING IN SARAH'S CAR WITH DIRTY PANTS

'Do you remember Mum's old friend from school?' I ask. 'She came to stay with us for a week. What was her name?'

'Sarah,' replies Louisa, who is still sitting next to me on my bed. 'She lives in Portugal.'

'Yes. She took me and you to the zoo one day.'

'That's right. You had an accident in her car on the way back.'

I shake my head. 'No, I didn't. That's just what I told Mum when we got home. I'd already done it before we got back in the car.'

'You had?' exclaims Louisa. 'When?'

'Just after Sarah bought us ice-creams.'

'But we stayed at the zoo for another hour

after that. Were you messy all that time?'

I nod. 'It was horrible, walking around the zoo, knowing that my pants were dirty. I had to try not to get too close to you or Sarah so you wouldn't smell it. And hope that nobody else in the zoo did either.'

'Why didn't you tell Sarah you'd had an accident? You know that Mum had given her spare pants and trousers and wipes for you, just in case.'

'Do you think Sarah expected a 7 year old boy to poo his pants? She probably just thought that I might wet myself if I got over excited, or was too shy to tell her I needed the toilet. I bet she wouldn't have taken me to the zoo if she thought she might have a pooey bum to clean. Just like our aunts and uncles won't have me over without Mum or Dad.'

'You could be right,' says Louisa. 'She probably didn't expect you to have an accident at all. Just thought that Mum was being really careful.'

'Right,' I say. 'And I certainly wasn't going to tell a grown-up I barely knew that I'd pooed myself. And then ask her to change my pants. No way!'

Louisa nods. 'I guess it would have been

really embarrassing for you.'

'Sure would,' I say. 'I know it was naughty to get back in her car wearing dirty pants. But what choice did I have? I'm just glad it was my turn to sit in the back seat. Sarah would have smelled it right away if I'd been sitting next to her.'

'She did smell something. Remember how she said, "I think someone should have gone to the toilet before we left the zoo," when we were half-way home?'

'Yeah, I was really scared she was going to stop the car and check my pants to see if I'd pooed in them. But she just thought one of us was farting a lot!'

Chapter 12
SURVIVING THE SNIFF TEST

There is silence in my bedroom for a minute. I think of another time when I nearly got caught with dirty pants by a grown-up I didn't know. Mum had left me at a story and crafts day at the local library. Just after one of the librarians had started reading the first story, my body told me to poo. I ignored it and carried on listening. I'd use the toilet when I got home, I thought. But it seemed that my body was in a hurry to get rid of my poo. By the time we got to the last story I had dirty pants. I gradually moved away from the other children sitting on the carpet and hoped that no-one would smell it.

I sat alone eating my sandwiches and drinking my orange squash during the lunch break. Then I went to the toilet for a wee and looked at my pants. They were quite messy.

I'd have to make sure that I didn't sit too near the other kids or the people who worked at the library, I thought. It was a big library and I should be able to find a place to sit by myself. I pulled my dirty pants back up and left the toilets.

That's another thing Mum and Dad can't understand. They don't know how I could pull my pants back up when I can see that they're messy. Of course, I wish they weren't messy. Of course, I'd rather be pulling clean pants back up. But I wasn't going to tell the librarians that I'd pooed myself. So I had to carry on wearing my dirty pants.

Once I tried to flush my pants down the toilet. But they blocked it up and it took Mum ages to sort it out. It was another thing I had to promise never to do again.

I couldn't sit on my own for the craftwork. We all had to sit around a large table. And it wasn't very long before one of the librarians noticed that the air didn't smell very fresh. 'Phew,' he said, 'has someone got messy pants?'

All the kids looked up from their pictures and models. A few of them giggled, but nobody said anything. I certainly wasn't going to admit to 20 other kids what I'd done. Especially as I was one of the oldest ones there.

The other librarian then asked, 'Has somebody pooed in their pants?' Nobody answered her either.

Then, to my horror, she got up and started asking the younger kids to stand up one at a time. When they did, she sniffed at their bottom through their clothes to see if they were smelly. 'Nobody's in trouble,' she said. 'Just need to see if someone has had a little accident and needs changing.'

I sat there waiting for it to be my turn to stand up and have my bum sniffed. I looked down miserably at the sticker on my t-shirt with my name and Mum's mobile phone number on it. I guessed that the number would soon be called and my Mum would be asked to come in to change me or take me home.

But I was never asked to stand up. The librarian didn't check anyone who looked older than 5. She must have thought that it couldn't have been one of the older kids who had messy pants. Like Sarah, she decided that it must just be a lot of farts she could smell. 'Well, please go to the toilet if you need to poo,' she said. 'If anyone can't wipe their own bottom, then please tell me and I'll come with you and do it for you.' One little boy immediately put up his hand and said he needed a poo and he needed help wiping. As he was led away from the table, I wondered if he'd also been trying to hold it in until he got home, because he couldn't wipe himself and was too shy to ask for help.

And all the time I sat there in dirty pants, I was afraid that the librarians would change their minds and decide to sniff test the older kids after all. Or for one of my neighbours to say that the boy sitting next to them really stank. I couldn't wait for the event to end and my Mum to take me home.

Louisa asks, 'Don't you find wearing messy pants uncomfortable?'

I shrug. 'Not really. I think I'm used to them.'

'It feels as normal as wearing clean pants?'

'Almost,' I reply. 'But I hate knowing that my pants are dirty. And if I don't tell anyone that I've had an accident, then I can pretend it hasn't happened. I know my dirty pants aren't going to go away if I ignore them. But I can pretend they're clean, pretend I'm a normal kid who always uses the toilet, not a baby who poos himself all the time.'

'You *are* a normal kid,' says Louisa, 'and you're not a baby.'

'Thanks,' I say, 'but I'd bet you'd rather have a different brother who didn't poo his pants.'

'Don't be stupid. I love my little brother, whether he's clean or messy. I wouldn't swap him for anyone else.'

This means so much to me. Without giving her any warning, I wrap my arms around Louisa and give her a huge hug! She deserves it. She's the best big sister in all the world!

Don't forget about Number 1!

If you often put off going to the toilet to do a wee for a long time, you can damage your kidneys and bladder.

Listen to your bladder, even when you're busy

Chapter 13
TUMMY ACHE

It's Friday after school and I'm sitting on my bed in pain. I've got a really bad tummy ache. It hurts so much. I'm holding my tummy and wishing the pain would go away.

I get a lot of tummy aches. They're always really painful and I hate them. But this is the worst one I've had for a long time.

I'm not going to tell Mum about it. 'When did you last go to the toilet?' she'll ask. Whatever answer I give, she'll still do the same thing. She'll make me sit on the toilet for ages and tell me to try to do a poo.

Last time she made me sit there for hours and hours. Well, it seemed like it was. In the end I did a very small poo and she let me get off.

Like Dad, Mum won't let me do anything while I'm on the toilet. It will be really, really boring.

I don't think I've pooed for a long time. I

had an accident on Monday. Dad took me and Louisa to the cinema. During the film I badly needed to do a poo. Of course, I didn't want to use the toilets at the cinema. Or miss a bit of the movie. So I tried really hard to hold it in. But I couldn't. It came out.

It wasn't a really big accident, but Dad soon smelled that I had dirty pants. He had to take me to the cinema toilets to change me.

There were a couple of other kids in there. I don't think they smelled what I'd done. But one boy spotted my Dad taking me into the cubicle. 'Look,' he said, 'he still needs his Dad to go in the toilet with him.' That wasn't as bad as them knowing that I'd already done it in my pants, but it was still embarrassing. And I missed a really big bit of the film.

I haven't used the toilet since then. I just haven't felt I've needed to go at the right time. It's not my fault if my silly body keeps telling me to poo while I'm at school.

My tummy slowly starts to feel better. Thank goodness! Now I can read the new book I've got from the library. Well, one of them. I've got four out. I like reading!

Chapter 14
OH NO!

Another Saturday, another playdate at Oliver's house. We're in Oliver's bedroom. I've told Oliver about the bad tummy ache I had yesterday. Now I'm telling him all about the new book I'm reading. It's really good. Then we start pretending we're trying to solve a mystery, just like the kids in the story.

'Okay,' I say to Oliver, 'we'll meet at the old barn at midnight.'

'Midnight? That'll be really dark.'

'Yes. We have to be really brave. And bring torches so we can see.'

Oliver nods. 'Yes. And some Wagon Wheels in case we get hungry. And some lemonade in case we get thirsty.'

'Right. And then we have to find a good hiding place. So the robbers can't see us. But we can hear them.'

'Okay. And then we'll find out which

bank they're planning to rob.'

'Yes,' I say. 'And then we can tell the police so they can catch them.'

'Super!' exclaims Oliver. 'And the police will say they've been trying to catch these crooks for years. And they'll give us medals. And a ride in a police car.'

'Right,' I say as I stand up. 'Let's look at the map.' I pull an invisible map out of my pocket. And then it happens.

I begin to wee.

Oh no! I look down in horror as I feel my wee starting to run down my legs. Stare at my light blue trousers as large areas change to a much darker colour. And then watch as I begin to make a big puddle on the carpet.

I'm frozen to the spot as I carry on weeing, unable to stop. It's been ages since I wet myself. At least three and a bit weeks. And I've never done it in front of Oliver before. I've never even told him that it sometimes happens. I didn't want him to think that I was totally unable to use the toilet.

Oliver is staring open mouthed at me. Then he jumps up and starts running downstairs. 'Mum,' he calls, 'Toby's wetting himself.'

I fall down on my knees as I finally stop weeing. My trousers are soaked and there's a large wet patch on the carpet. I put my head in my hands. Oliver's going to think I'm a complete baby now. One who both poos and wees in his pants. Will he still want to be my friend after this?

Chapter 15
BE BRAVE, TOBY

I'm sitting on Oliver's bed after coming out of the bathroom. I hadn't brought spare trousers with me, so Oliver's Mum has let me borrow a pair of Oliver's jeans. At least I'm dry again now. I can change myself when I'm only wet. Last year, Mum tried to get me to do it when I had dirty pants as well. But I made such a mess in the bathroom that she changed her mind.

Oliver and his Mum peek into the room and then come inside. They sit on either side of me on the bed.

'Feeling better?' asks Oliver's Mum.

'A bit,' I reply. I look at the damp patch on the floor. 'I'm sorry.'

Oliver's Mum follows my gaze. 'Don't worry about the carpet, I can wash it. It's the second time it's been wee'd on this month.'

I look across at Oliver. 'It wasn't me!' he exclaims.

'It was one of Oliver's little cousins,' says his Mum. 'He wet his pants while Oliver was playing with him.'

'You must think I'm a complete baby,' I say to Oliver. 'I don't suppose you want to be my friend anymore.'

'Of course I still want to be your friend,' he replies. 'And I don't think you're a baby.'

'And neither do I,' says his Mum. 'I think you're a great kid who has a little problem using the toilet. Tell me, Toby, did you know you needed to wee before you did it?'

I shake my head. 'I never do when I wet myself. Mum says it's when I have a big poo stuck inside me and it pushes on that thing, oh, what's it called? That bag in my body where I keep my wee until I go to the toilet.'

'Your bladder?'

'That's it, my bladder. And then I just start to wee and I can't stop.'

'Okay, Toby,' says Oliver's Mum, 'I understand what happened. Right, shall we do something to try to stop it from happening again?'

I stare at her. 'What do you mean?'

'Well, if you've got a big poo in you, why don't you try to get it out?'

'You mean...try to use the toilet?'

'Yes. And I don't mean when you get home. Why don't you try to use the toilet here?'

I shake my head. 'I can't. I can't poo in toilets in other people's houses.'

'Why not?'

'I just can't.'

Oliver's Mum is quiet for a moment. Then she asks, 'Toby, are you going to spend the rest of your life avoiding using the toilet in other people's homes? Or at school? Or in shops, or in restaurants or at theme parks? Do you want to be having accidents when you're 10? Or 13? Or 16?'

'No,' I reply. I know a lot of older kids still have toilet problems. And a lot of teenagers. But I don't want to be one of them.

'Well, why don't we see if we can do something to stop them from happening. We have a pretty nice bathroom here, don't we?'

'Yes.'

'So let's take that first step in helping you to overcome your problems. I know I'm asking you to do a lot. I know this is a big deal for you. But I'm confident that you can do it. Be brave, Toby.'

'I'll sit in the bathroom with you,' says

Oliver. 'We can play the Alphabet Game.'

Can I? Can I really try to do a poo at Oliver's house?

Be brave, Toby.

'Okay,' I say, 'I'll try.'

Chapter 16
THE BIGGEST, SMELLIEST POO IN THE WORLD

Oliver has brought a small chair into the bathroom. He sits on it while I sit on the toilet. When we were younger we used to go to the toilet together when one of us needed to wee, but never for poos. It seems a bit strange to be doing it now. But it's nice to have a friend with me while I'm trying to poo in his toilet for the first time ever.

We're playing the Alphabet Game with animals. You take it in turns trying to think of animals starting with the letter A. If you can't think of another animal then the other person gets a point. Then you move on to letter B. Then letter C. Then…oh, I think you get the idea!

'A for adder,' I say.

'A for aardvark,' says Oliver.

'What's that?' I ask.

'It comes from Africa. It eats ants. Your turn.'

But I can't think of another animal starting with A. We've already named about a hundred each. Okay, maybe about five each. 'I give up.'

'My point,' says Oliver. 'Okay, B for bear.'

I start to feel something move when we get to D. I gently push. When we get to F I feel that my poo is getting ready to come out. I carry on pushing.

And while Oliver is trying to think of an animal starting with J, my poo starts to come out of my bottom. I can tell that it's going to be a very big poo. 'It's coming!' I say to Oliver.

He seems as excited as me. 'Great! Go for it, Toby!'

I carry on pushing my poo out. 'Watch out,' I say, 'it's going to get very smelly in here soon.'

'I don't mind if you stink up the bathroom,' says Oliver. 'I've done it hundreds of times. That's what it's here for. It's a lot better than stinking up my bedroom.'

We both hear a loud plop as poo falls into the water in the toilet below me. Oliver cheers. But I know there's more to come. I carry on pushing.

Oliver runs downstairs to fetch his Mum. More poo comes out of me and falls into the toilet. But I'm still not finished. I grip the sides of the toilet seat and keep pushing.

'Wow, it stinks in here!' says Oliver's Mum as she comes into the bathroom with Oliver. 'Well done, Toby! I'm proud of you.'

'I'm not finished yet,' I say, and have one last push. The final piece of poo falls out of my bottom and makes a really loud plop. That's it! I've got it all out. 'All done!' I say. I get off the toilet. Bum wiping can wait for a minute. I want Oliver and his Mum to see what I've done.

'Goodness, Toby,' says Oliver's Mum, 'did you have all that in your body? No wonder you had a tummy ache yesterday. I'm amazed that a 7 year old boy could do that. It's the biggest poo I've ever seen.'

'I think it's the biggest poo in all the world,' says Oliver, 'and the smelliest!'

His Mum gets out her mobile phone and starts sending a text. 'I'm going to tell your parents about this monster poo,' she says. 'I'm sure they'll be proud of you for using the toilet at my house. You should be proud of yourself as well. And you should be proud of that poo.'

I look down again at my poo. It was definitely one to be proud of. And I'm so glad that I did it in the toilet and not in my pants. I wouldn't have liked to have walked around with all that poo in my underwear. I would have been the Incredibly Stinky Kid!

Instead I've stank up Oliver's Mum's bathroom. And I'm proud of myself for doing that

Pooed in the toilet? Well done! Now wipe from front to back!

> Hi! This advice is really important for girls, so please tell your sisters and girls you know.

> It's so the germs in her poo don't get near where her wee comes out.

It's good advice for boys as well!

Don't be back to front!
Wipe FRONT to BACK!

Chapter 17
A DIRTY PULL-UP AND A HAPPY MUM

On Monday I had an accident at school. I think Mum was disappointed when she came in to change me. Come on, Mum, just because I pooed at Oliver's house, I'm not going to start pooing in the school toilets, am I?

It's now Thursday. I've been holding my poo in at school since just before lunchtime. I was going to use the toilet as soon as I got home, really I was. But Mum and Dad have decided that we need to go shopping. So we all came to Asda straight after school. We didn't even go home first so that me and Louisa could take off our uniforms.

The customer toilets are just inside the store. I look at them for a second. Should I ask Dad to take me to the toilet? No. Sorry, but I can't use shop toilets. Not for a poo, anyway. I'll just have to try and hold it in until we get home.

It seems strange walking around Asda in my school uniform and wearing a pull-up. I really, really hope that I can keep it clean until we get home.

But I can't.

We're in the fresh fruit section and Mum sends me to get some bananas. I see a nice bunch and reach for it. And that's when it happens. I can't hold my poo in any longer. It comes out into my pull-up. Oh no!

What am I going to do? We've only just started shopping. We've got to go all the way around the store. And then pay for our groceries. I won't be able to keep my dirty pull-up a secret all that time. Mum or Dad or Louisa is bound to smell it soon. It won't be long before one of them finds out that I've had an accident.

I suddenly have a crazy idea. Why don't I tell Mum? I know it will be really embarrassing. But at least I won't have to walk around Asda in a dirty pull-up that other grown-ups and kids can smell, before Mum or Dad find out anyway. And at least Mum won't have to sniff at my trousers or look in my pull-up to check if I'm messy.

I pick-up the bananas and start to walk back to Mum. Be brave, Toby. You can tell her.

I hand the bananas to Mum. 'Thanks, love,' she says, and turns to put the bananas in the trolley.

I pull at her coat sleeve. 'Mum?'

She turns and looks down at me. 'Yes, darling?'

I pause, bite my lip for a second, and then I say it. 'My pull-up is dirty.'

Mum actually smiles at me. Then she kneels down to me. She's still smiling. 'Thank you for telling me, Toby. That makes me really happy.'

'It does?' I say, surprised.

'Yes. I know that must have been really hard for you. That was a really brave thing to do.' She stands up. 'Right, we'll go back to the car and get your changing bag. The toilets are just inside the doors, so hardly anyone will see it. And then we'll get you cleaned up. Okay?'

I nod happily. Now that I've told Mum, I just can't wait to get out of this dirty, smelly pull-up.

Mum tells Dad what's going on. He's going to carry on shopping with Louisa until we get back.

'Come on, my big brave boy,' says Mum, offering her hand. 'Let's go back to the car park and then get you changed.'

I take her hand and we head back towards the entrance. I don't care if other shoppers can smell me as we walk past them. I don't care if they know what I've done. My mother is happy with me and thinks I'm a big, brave boy. And I've never been so happy in a dirty pull-up!

I'm really glad I told Mum.

Chapter 18
THE NEW BABYSITTER

It's Friday evening and Mum and Dad are going out. Mum's found a new babysitter to look after me and Louisa. She's called Gemma.

She's a bit older than Tina and she smiles a lot more. 'Hello,' she says when she first sees me, 'you must be Toby.'

'Yes, I am.' I say.

'Well, hi Toby. I'm Gemma. I'm your new babysitter. I hope we're going to have lots of fun together. I enjoy playing whatever you enjoy playing.'

She must enjoy playing lots of things then, because I do!

Gemma goes on, 'And your Mum's told me that you have problems doing your number 2s and you sometimes have an accident in your pants. Don't worry, I've dealt with lots of pooey bottoms over the years.'

'Have you?' I ask.

'Yes,' says Gemma. 'Mostly babies and toddlers, but I don't mind cleaning big kids' bums as well. Last year I looked after a 6 year old girl who had the same problem as you. I often had to change her pants. And I used to work in a school. There was an 8 year old boy in one class who had to wear pull-ups because he had a lot of accidents, both wee and poo. He usually changed himself, but I had to help him when he was really messy.'

'I have to wear pull-ups at school,' I tell Gemma. 'And I sometimes wet myself when I have a big poo inside me.'

'I know, your Mum told me that as well. That's okay, I don't mind mopping up puddles on the floor either. But will you do something for me, Toby? Will you tell me if you have an accident and you need me to change you? I promise I won't be cross with you or shout at you. Will you do that?'

I nod. 'I promise.' And I mean to keep this promise. I'll tell Gemma straight away if I need changing.

'Good,' says Gemma, 'that would be a really big kid thing to do. And the quicker we can get you cleaned up, the quicker we

81

can go back to having fun.'

I like Gemma. She seems really nice. And it's great to have my babysitter call me a big kid instead of a big baby.

'Right,' says Gemma, 'it's time to play. What would you like to do first?'

Are you drinking enough?

> When I go to the toilet, my wee is dark yellow.

> You're not drinking enough. Your wee should be light yellow, almost like water.

> Drink 6 - 8 glasses of water, squash or juice every day.

> This will help your bladder to fill and stretch so it can hold more wee and stay healthy. It will also help your poo to keep moving!

What colour is YOUR wee?

Chapter 19
A TOILET SIT AND AN IDEA

'Something's coming!' I exclaim. I push. Gemma stops reading. Seconds later I tell her, 'I'm doing a poo!'

'Brilliant!' says Gemma. 'Clever boy!'

After Gemma had washed up the teatime dishes she asked me if I wanted to sit on the toilet. 'It's a good time to try to do a poo,' she said. 'You can often do one after you've eaten, even if you didn't know you wanted to. '

I didn't think I needed to poo, but I agreed to try.

Gemma seemed really pleased. She came into the bathroom and sat on the side of the bath while I sat on the toilet. She read *James and the Giant Peach* to me while I gently pushed and tried to do a poo.

Nothing happened for ten minutes, but I

enjoyed the story. And then I felt myself starting to poo.

After I've done it, I look down into the toilet bowl. It's not a big poo, but I'm still pleased that I did it in the toilet instead of in my pants. 'Well, I don't think I'm going to have an accident tonight!' I tell Gemma.

'Yes,' she agrees. 'it looks like we're going to be pooey bum free this evening. Well done, Toby! Doing a toilet sit when you didn't think you needed to poo was a really big kid thing to do. You should be proud of yourself.'

'Can you send a text and tell Mum and Dad about it?' I ask.

'Sure.' She gets out her mobile phone and starts tapping away on the keyboard. 'I'm also telling them how you agreed to do a toilet sit without any arguments, and what a good boy you've been this evening. They're going to be so pleased with you, Toby.'

I sit on the toilet happily while Gemma finishes her message.

'All done,' she says, and puts away her phone. 'Okay, do you need any help wiping your bottom? I don't mind if you do. Lots of kids can't wipe themselves. Especially if they have poo problems like you.'

'It's okay, I can do it,' I say, reaching for the paper. I've been able to wipe my own bum since I was 4. Well, 4 and a bit. Okay, 4 and a very big bit.

'That's great, it's a very useful skill to have. Especially at school.'

I nod as I wipe myself. I don't tell her that I have never, ever pooed in the school toilets and I never, ever will.

As we're walking back down the stairs, I start to think. I'm not going to poo at school, but perhaps I could start using the toilets in other places. Like in shops and places we visit. Such as when we go to the PlayAway kids' centre. I know the toilets there are nice. And I'm getting tired of other parents staring at me when Mum or Dad has to take me into the Parent & Baby Room there after I've had an accident.

I nearly always need changing at some point when we go for a day out. Sometimes more than once. I'm fed up of having dirty pants every time we go somewhere. And I'm really fed up of having to be changed in public toilets, or in baby changing rooms. If I told Mum or Dad that I needed the toilet when I felt I had to poo, then I wouldn't have an accident. I wouldn't be messy. I wouldn't be smelly. I wouldn't need changing. And I wouldn't have to pretend that I was clean when I wasn't.

It sounds like a good idea to me! But could I do it? Would I really be able to use the toilet for a poo on a day out?

Chapter 20
A POO AT THE MUSEUM

It's Sunday, and Mum and Dad have brought me and Louisa to a toy museum. It's huge and filled with thousands of toys and games from the past.

There's hundreds of teddy bears, lead soldiers, stuffed toys, dolls and dolls houses, board games, jigsaws and toys for outdoors. A lot of them are just to look at, but some of them you can play with.

In the middle of the ground floor there's the trunk of a tree. It isn't a real tree, but it looks pretty real. It rises up from the floor and goes up into the ceiling. 'What's that doing here?' I ask.

Dad smiles. 'You'll see when we go upstairs.'

And I do see! In the middle of the next floor is a tree house with branches of the not real tree hanging over it. I guess you could get about six kids in there. Inside are a few books and toys and drawing and colouring materials.

Dad says that me and Louisa can go inside the tree house for a while. There are already three children in there. We go through the entrance and join them.

Louisa whispers in my ear. 'I hope you don't have an accident in here. You'll stink up the tree house in no time.'

'I hope I don't have an accident all day,' I whisper back. But I'm already a bit nervous about what I'm planning to do. I just hope they have nice toilets here. I start to draw a picture of the not real tree and tree house. Louisa plays with some strange toy that she says is called a Rubik's Cube.

After half an hour Mum says we have to come out so that other children can have a turn. I need a wee anyway. I tell Mum and she takes me to the family toilets they have here for both boys and girls to use.

The toilets are really nice and clean. There are none of those toilets that nobody can poo in and only boys can wee in, just lots of regular toilets. There are quite a few kids in there, as well as Mums and Dads. Some parents go into the cubicles to help kids who are too young to go by themselves. Others are waiting outside for older children.

One of the cubicle doors opens and a little girl comes out with her Dad. 'I've done a big poo-poo,' she says proudly in a loud voice, 'and my Daddy wiped my bum!' She looks about 3. Maybe 3 and a bit. Or 3 and a half. Perhaps 3 and a half and a bit.

'Okay, Lily, not everyone wants to know,' says her Dad. But he looks very pleased with his daughter as he helps her to wash and dry her hands.

After I've done a wee and washed my own hands we all go up the stairs to the next floor. In the middle of this floor there's a special display of video games from the 1980s. I know, pre-historic! There are loads of them, and you're allowed to play on any one you like. There a lot of children playing already, but there are still a few spaces. Me and Louisa definitely want to have a go!

Some of the games are quite simple, but they're still fun. I play Donkey Kong for a bit, then a game called Manic Miner. And then it happens. My body tells me I need to poo.

Okay, this is it. Be brave, Toby. If that little girl can do a poo in the family toilets, then so can I. I get up and walk over to where Mum and Dad are looking at the covers of some comics that are really, really old. My changing bag is resting against one of the legs of the display case. Well, it can stay there!

'I want to go to the toilet,' I say to them.

'Are you sure?' asks Dad. 'You went less than half an hour ago.'

'That was for a wee,' I tell him. 'Now I want to do a poo.'

Both Mum and Dad's mouths drop open. They look at each other. They appear to be shocked. Then Mum turns back to me and says, 'Oh Toby, I'm so proud of you. You've just made me the happiest Mum here.'

'And I'm proud of you too, Toby,' says Dad, 'well done!'

'Would you like to take him to the toilet?' Mum asks Dad.

'Nothing would give me more pleasure than taking my son to do a poo,' says Dad, and I know that he really means it. He looks as pleased as Lily's Dad did after his daughter had done a poo. But my Dad won't be wiping my bum!

'Right,' says Mum, 'and I'll take his changing bag back to the car. It looks like we're not going to need it today. '

I feel a bit scared as Dad takes my hand and we start to walk back to the family toilets. But I'm not chickening out now! I have to poo and this time it's going in the toilet, not in my pants!

Public toilets won't bite your bum!

> Some adults try to avoid doing a poo (or even a wee) in pubic toilets.

> That's nonsense! Don't try to hold on until you get home. Get into good habits while you're still a kid.

Show the grown-ups how it's done!

Chapter 21
MEETING A GIRL WHO POOED HER PANTS

As I walk back to the video games I see that there is now a space at the console next to Louisa. She is talking to the girl sitting on the other side of her. The girl looks about the same age as Louisa.

I sit at the console next to my sister. 'Hi Louisa,' I say, 'I'm back.'

'Where have you been?' she asks me.

'I've been to the toilet,' I tell her. 'I did a poo.'

She turns to face me, a look of delight on her face. She doesn't even mind when the ghosts promptly catch her Pac-Man. 'That's brilliant,' she says. 'Well done, little brother.'

The girl sitting next to her overhears us. 'Why are you saying well done to him?' she asks. 'What's so brilliant about doing a poo?'

Louisa turns to face the girl. Tell her to mind her own business, I think.

But it seems that Louisa does not want to be rude to her new friend. 'It's a big deal for him,' she explains. 'He has problems with his poos.'

'Problems?' asks the girl. 'What sort of problems?'

'Well, he sometimes has accidents. In his pants.'

Thank you, Louisa, I think. Tell this girl my embarrassing secret, why don't you? My sister has just gone and ruined my day for me. And I was feeling so good about myself. I wait for the other girl to laugh and make fun of me.

But she doesn't. 'I used to poo my knickers sometimes,' she says.

'You did?' asks Louisa.

'Yeah. I didn't like using the girls toilets at school. Or toilets at places like this. So I tried to hold my poo in. It worked for a little while, but I kept making a mess in my knickers. Sometimes just a little mess, but sometimes a great big one. So I stopped doing it. Made myself go to the toilet, any toilet, whenever I needed to poo.' She looks at me. 'Well done,' she says, and she sounds like she means it. Then she goes back to playing Centipede.

Wow! I've just met a girl who used to poo her pants. I knew that there were other kids out there who had accidents like I do, but I never thought I would meet one. She tried to hold in her poo instead of going to the toilet. Just like I do. And then she pooed her pants. Just like I do. But she doesn't try to avoid using the toilet anymore. And she's stopped having accidents. So maybe I can too.

Louisa starts a new game of Pac-Man and I decide to try playing Buggy Boy. I'm really enjoying myself now. Not only because the games are great fun. But also because I'm not worried that I'm going to have an accident while we're here. I'm not thinking that at some point I might be playing these games while wearing dirty pants. I'm not going to have to pretend that I'm clean when I know that I'm messy. I won't have to move away from my sister so she doesn't smell my poo. I won't have to worry about other kids guessing what I've done. And I won't have Mum or Dad checking my pants and then taking me off to change me.

Using the toilet is much better than holding in my poo! I feel great!

Using the toilet is much better than holding in my poo! I feel great!

Chapter 22
CAN I DO A POO IN THE SCHOOL TOILETS?

Oh no! It's Wednesday morning, I'm in school and I need to poo.

It's really early, school only started twenty minutes ago. I don't think I'm going to be able to hold my poo in all day until I go home. I'm going to have an accident. My first accident since I pooed myself in Asda on Thursday. Hopefully Mum won't be too disappointed when she comes in to change me.

It's horrible sitting in the classroom, knowing that I'll have a dirty pull-up before the end of the day. I haven't done a poo since we went to the toy museum on Sunday. So when I have an accident it's going to be a big one. Everyone in the class will probably smell it. And so will everyone who passes me in the corridor while I'm waiting for

Mum to arrive. They'll all know that I've pooed my pull-up again. But there's nothing I can do about it.

Unless…

Could I do it? Could I actually ask to go to the boys toilets? Could I do a poo there like I did in the museum?

I remember the girl sitting next to Louisa at the video games. She used to avoid using the toilets at school, but she got over it. Could I do the same thing?

I also remember what Oliver's Mum said to me after I wet myself at her house. Do I still want to be wearing pull-ups to school when I'm 10? Or when I'm a teenager? Do I want to be having accidents in the classroom when I'm 16?

Then I look over to where Lucy is sitting and remember what happened to her in assembly last year. Lucy must have known that she needed a wee because she was fidgeting so much. She could have told a teacher that she wanted to go to the toilet. But she didn't. She just sat there until she wet herself. Was I going to do the same thing? Was I just going to sit here until I pooed myself?

No, I wasn't!

It was time to be a big kid. It was time to do the right thing. It was time to go to the toilet.

I take a deep breath. Be brave, Toby. You can do this.

I put up my hand. Mrs Mattock spots it straight away. 'Yes, Toby?'

Another breath. Then I ask, 'Can I go to the toilet, please?'

'No, you may not go to the toilet, Toby,' replies Mrs Mattock. 'The school day only started twenty minutes ago. If you went to the toilet before you left home or when you arrived at school, then you should not need to go again so soon.'

Oh no! It took all my courage to ask and now Mrs Mattock has said no.

A girl sitting near me sniggers. 'He'll have to go toilet in his pull-up,' she says to her neighbour.

No! That is not going to happen today. I put my hand up again.

'Yes, Toby,' says Mrs Mattock wearily.

'I do have to go to the toilet, Mrs Mattock,' I say. 'I need to poo and I don't want to do it in my pull-up.'

There are gasps around the room. Some of my classmates can't believe that I've said that. Neither can I!

Mrs Mattock smiles at me. 'In that case, Toby, of course you may go to the toilet.'

REMEMBER, EVERYBODY POOS!
(INCLUDING TEACHERS!)

If you need to poo, you know what to do!

Put up your hand and go to the loo!

It's COOL to POO at SCHOOL!

Chapter 23
THE HAPPIEST BOY IN THE SCHOOL

I've done it! I've done my first ever poo in the boys toilets. It wasn't as massive as the one I did at Oliver's house, but it was big and it was smelly! I can't wait to tell Mum that I've done my first school toilet poo when she picks me up at going home time.

I wipe my bottom and pull up my pull-up. Then I flush and leave the cubicle.

Two older boys come into the toilets while I'm drying my hands after washing them. 'Phew, what a stink!' says one of them. He looks at me with disgust. 'I bet he's done a poo.'

'Dirty little stinker!' says his friend.

I put my head down and walk to the exit. But I stop as I reach the door. I'm not going to let these two boys ruin this moment for me. I turn around, lift up my head and look the first boy in the face. 'Yes, I have,' I tell him. 'I've done a big, smelly poo in the school toilets. And I'm proud of it. What do you think I should have done? Pooed my pants? Well, I'm not going to do that at school ever again.' And then I open the door and leave the boys toilets, still holding my head high.

It was worth it to see the shocked expression on that boy's face. I start to walk back towards my classroom, happy to leave the poo smell in the boys toilets instead of carrying it around with me.

It's great knowing that when I get back to my seat, I'm not going to have an accident today. No-one is going to tell Mrs Mattock that I stink. I'm not going to have to sit outside the office smelling of poo. And my Mum is not going to have to come into school to change me.

As I push open the door to the classroom, I decide that right now I'm probably the happiest boy in the school.

Chapter 24
NO MORE STINKY KID!

'Mum,' I say as I run up to where she is standing near the school gates, 'I've done a poo.' Yes, I really couldn't wait to tell her!

Mum smiles at me. 'Okay darling, thank you for telling me. We'd better take you back inside and get you clean before we go home.'

Get me clean? What does Mum mean? And then I realise. She thinks I've had an accident. 'I haven't done it in my pull-up,' I tell her. 'I did it in the boys toilets. This morning. Just after school started.'

Mum looks even more surprised than when I told her I needed to poo at the toy museum. Next thing I know she picks me up and starts spinning me around! 'Oh you clever, clever boy,' she says. 'What a big, brave thing for you to do. You've made me really, really happy. I'm so proud of you.'

The other parents who were picking up

their kids must have wondered what on earth I'd done to deserve such praise!

While we are walking home, I tell Mum all about what happened. How I was going to try to hold it in and then changed my mind. How Mrs Mattock told me I couldn't go to the toilet, but I wasn't taking no for an answer.

'I told the whole class that I needed to poo,' I say to Mum, 'and I didn't care that they knew. I just wanted to get to the toilets and not do it in my pull-up.'

'Good for you!' says Mum. 'Remember, every child in that class also poos, and so does Mrs Mattock. Every single person in the whole world poos.'

I go on to tell Mum about the two older boys who complained about the smell in the boys toilets, and what I said to them.

'That's great!' says Mum. 'Well done for standing up for yourself. What silly boys! It sounds like they should probably still be wearing nappies!'

'I'm always going to use the school toilets from now on,' I say, 'every time I need to poo or wee. Using the toilet is much better than trying to hold my poo in. And it's much, much, much better than having an accident and being stinky in the classroom. And having to wear pull-ups and have my Mum come into school to change me. Going to the toilet is great!'

'I'm glad you think so, Toby. I can't believe what a big, brave, clever son I've got. Whatever happened to the Nappy Boy and the Stinky Kid?'

'I'm going to be the Toilet Boy instead, because I'm always going to the toilet!' I reply. Okay, I don't really want that nickname. But I know one thing for sure. I'm not going to be the Stinky Kid anymore!

Chapter 25
I'M PROUD OF MY POOS!

Louisa comes upstairs after she gets back from after school football practice. 'Toby,' she says as she comes into my bedroom without bothering to ask first, 'Mum told me that you pooed at school today.'

'That's right. I did a big, smelly poo in the boys toilets and it felt great.'

'Way to go, little brother! Give me five!'

We high-five, then I tell her all about it, just like I told Mum.

'That's great,' she says, 'I knew you'd do it one day. And I think if you can poo at school then you can poo anywhere, in any toilet.'

'Really?' There's still some public toilets I don't want to use. Like the ones in St Ann's Park. They're made of metal and they don't smell very nice. I don't even use them when I need to wee. I go behind a tree instead.

'Sure thing,' says Louisa. 'Lots of kids don't like using school toilets, especially for poos. Some of my friends don't. They don't have accidents, but they don't use the toilets at school unless they really have to. That's just silly. If I need to poo at school, then I go to the toilet and poo.'

'So will I from now on,' I say. 'Every single time.'

'Go for it, it's cool to poo at school! Some kids don't even like weeing at school. They don't drink much during the day so they don't have to use the toilet.'

'Mum says that's really bad for you. She tells me that I must make sure I drink enough water or juice every day.'

'She tells me that as well' says Louisa. 'You can damage your kidneys and bladder if you don't. Anyway, I'm really glad you stank up the boys toilets. Now I want you to stink up lots of other toilets. When we go shopping, when we go on days out, when we're at family parties. Everywhere!'

'But what about toilets that aren't very nice?' I ask. 'Like the ones in St Ann's Park?'

'Well, do you remember what happened when you had an accident in St Ann's Park? Mum had to change your pants in the park toilets, didn't she?'

I nod. That was so embarrassing. Mum had to take me into the Ladies toilets. There were quite a few girls in there. And there was a queue for the toilets. Not the best place to take a 7 year old boy who stank of poo and had a big brown patch on the back of his bright green shorts. Nearly all the girls laughed at me while we were queuing for a toilet.

And it really wasn't a very nice place to be changed. Especially as it took Mum forever to get me clean. I'd been running, jumping and playing in dirty pants for ages before she found out that I'd had an accident.

'Well,' Louisa goes on, 'don't you think being changed in not very nice toilets is worse than using them?'

'Yes,' I reply. I know she's right. But I also know that I'll have to be really brave to use some toilets. But I'll try. I never thought I'd poo in the school toilets and now I have.

'So, are you up for it?' asks Louisa.

'Yes! I'm going to do it. I'm going to stink up every toilet I can.'

'That's the spirit, boy. Stink up the loos! Be proud of your poos!'

'I'M PROUD OF MY POOS!' I shout, holding my arms in the air.

Then we both fall onto my bed, and collapse into fits of laughter.

MESSAGE BY TORCHLIGHT

Hi! I'm supposed to be going to sleep. So I'm writing this under my sheet, using the light from my torch. Don't tell Mum, will you? Promise?

Okay, so it's now two months since I first pooed in the school toilets. I've done lots and lots of poos at school since then. I'm always putting my hand up and asking if I can go to the toilet. Mrs Mattock doesn't mind. She's just glad she hasn't got the Stinky Kid in her class anymore! And I don't have to wear pull-ups to school now. That's great! I just have to remember that I can't do a sneaky wee in the classroom anymore! Oh, and I've been invited to Rory's birthday party next week!

I'm doing what I said. I've pooed in lots of

different toilets in the last two months. Some are really nice and some aren't so nice. But Louisa is right. It's better to use them than be changed in them. Last week I both wee'd and pooed in the toilets in St Ann's Park. They didn't smell very nice when I went in. But they smelled a lot worse when I came out! I think I really can poo in any toilet now!

I'm also doing toilet sits for ten minutes when Mum or Dad or Gemma ask me to. I even do it without being asked if I haven't pooed for a day or two. I'm now allowed to have a book to read while I'm sitting there, or I can watch a video or play a game on the tablet. Sometimes I poo during a toilet sit and sometimes I don't. But Mum and Dad and Gemma are always pleased with me when I try. Gemma doesn't sit in the bathroom with me anymore. Neither does Oliver. I think I might be a bit too old for that now. But I was really glad of their help when I needed it.

Sometimes, I find myself trying to hold my poo in, and I have to stop myself. Mum says it's because not going to the toilet has become a habit for me, and habits are hard to get out of. But she says that I can do it if I try really hard. So I'm trying really hard. If Mum or Dad see me holding my poo they suggest that I go to the toilet. And I always do. I don't want to go back to having a lot of accidents again. Even Louisa has spotted me holding a couple of times and told me I should go for a poo. I know it sounds embarrassing to have your sister tell you to go to the toilet when you're 7 years old, but I don't mind. It's much better than not using the toilet and doing it in my pants. Oh, and I don't get tummy aches anymore. And I haven't wet myself since I did it in Oliver's bedroom. Pretty good, huh?

I've only had two accidents in the last two months. One was when Mum and Dad were out. I said to Gemma, 'My pants are dirty.' and she was really pleased with me for telling her. The other time was at Auntie Fiona's house. Oh well, at least I didn't ruin her biscuit barrel this time! One day I'm going to call Auntie Fiona into her bathroom and show her a big, smelly poo that I've done in her toilet! I'm hoping that I'll have stopped having accidents altogether by the time I'm 8. But I think Auntie Fiona will still make me wear pull-ups to her house until I'm 88!

Are you still having accidents? If you are, then I hope you can soon become clean like I (nearly) am. Remember, you can't make your poo disappear. Don't try to hold it in, it's got to come out sometime. And I guess you'd much rather do it in the toilet than in your pants.

You probably hate having dirty pants as much as I did. Even if you can't tell that to a grown-up. And you probably find it just as hard as I did to tell someone when you've had an accident. Go on, be brave like me. Dirty pants won't go away by themselves. Change yourself, or tell a grown-up that you've pooed. Don't stay messy and smelly for ages like I used to do. Get yourself back in clean pants as soon as you can. It's much better for your health. And you'll feel much better as well.

And don't be frightened of school toilets. Or toilets in other people's houses, or in shops, or public toilets. They're all there to be pooed in and none of them will bite your bum. Go on, stink up every toilet you can!

Good luck! You can do it!

Oh, I think I can hear Mum coming upstairs to check on me. I'll have to switch my light out and pretend that I'm asleep.

Bye bye.

Toby

Good Luck!

You can do it!

ABOUT THE AUTHOR

James Parkin's first books for children were the *Ghost Gang* series, which featured a group of friendly ghosts who help the children who have problems at Claire Rock Primary School. He wrote these three books while at university, drawing on several years experience of doing voluntary work in various local primary schools, day nurseries and playgroups with children of all ages from 0 to 11. He brought out revised editions of these books in 2012.

James had encopresis as a child and often soiled himself until he was 11. At the time, and for several years afterwards, he thought he was the only school aged child in the world who still pooed his pants. Years later he was surprised to find letters on the problem pages in newspapers and magazines from worried parents whose children often soiled themselves, including an 11 year old girl who frequently messed her pants and, like him, couldn't explain why she did it. With the arrival of the internet James discovered just how widespread a problem soiling was among children and teenagers.

As an adult he has tried to use his experiences to help today's children and their parents who are struggling with this embarrassing condition. He has published two blogs, where his honest and candid discussion of his childhood soiling has been appreciated by many parents.

In 2014 he wrote a book for older children who soil their pants, which he republished two years later in separate editions for boys and girls called *A Boy Like You* and *A Girl Like You*. Many children who have poo accidents, and their parents, have found these books very useful, and they have been endorsed by the children's continence charity ERIC. In 2020 he wrote and published *Help! I Poo My Pants* for boys and girls aged 5 to 8 who withhold their poo instead of going to the toilet and then mess their pants, which he hopes will prove equally useful to younger children and their parents.

He has also written *News from the Loos*, a book of short stories for all children aged 7 to 11, to try to raise awareness and understanding of children's toilet problems and encourage good bladder and bowel health at school and elsewhere. He hopes that it is also a fun read for kids!

James is single, lives in the UK and has a First Class BA (Hons) degree in Education Studies and History from De Montfort University.

The author's blogs about his soiling problems

For parents

childhoodsoiling.blogspot.co.uk

For children

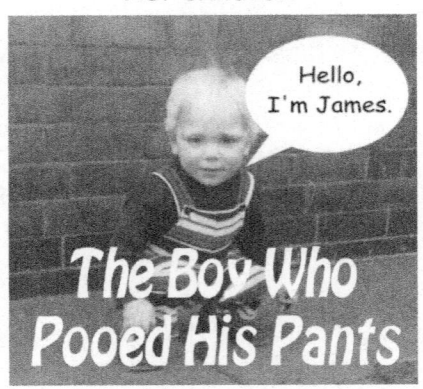

theboywhopooedhispants.blogspot.co.uk

FACEBOOK

There are several groups on Facebook for parents of children who soil. One of the largest groups, of which the author is a member and administrator, is called *HELP!!!! My Child Has Encopresis*. At the time of writing, this group had over 7,000 members across the globe.

The group is a great forum for posting ideas on what works and what doesn't for treating children's constipation and soiling problems, sharing success stories and letting off steam on bad days. No subject is TMI, and there is, naturally, much talk about poo, the toilet and soiled pants! Advice for dealing with schools and the medical profession is also regularly sought and offered, and matters which may be related to encopresis are also dealt with, such as wetting problems and behavioural issues.

For many parents simply being among others who are raising an encopretic child is a great support and comfort, as is the ability to discuss matters they feel they cannot talk about with their family and friends.

The author would like to thank the group for their support for these books, and their help in some of the phrasing for the American editions.

Other Facebook groups for parents set up by the author

Daytime Wetting in Children and Teens

Bedwetting in Children and Teens

Also available by the same author

A boy like you

A girl like you

A story for older children who soil their pants

Recommended age 8 to 12 years

For details please go to
www.bigredsock.com

Also available by the same author

Come and join us in the toilets!

NEWS from the LOOS

Stories from the School Toilets

"Hi, I'm Penny Spender, Librarian and School Toilets Reporter! Join me and the kids of Parktree Primary School as we tell you tales from the new Key Stage 2 unisex loos. Find amusing, sometimes embarrassing, stories in this fun book for all kids aged 7 to 11."

For details please go to
www.bigredsock.com

Also available by the same author

GHOST GANG

The New Ghost
Helen's Heartaches
Complicated Creatures

Come and meet Claire Rock Primary School's friendly ghosts!

Recommended reading age 8 to 12 years

*Available in paperback
and for the Kindle and Kindle apps
from Amazon*

ERIC
The Children's Bowel and Bladder Charity

The UK based charity ERIC (Education and Resources for Improving Childhood Continence) is unique in focusing on all aspects of childhood toilet issues: potty training, bedwetting, daytime wetting, constipation and soiling.

Based in Bristol, ERIC offer a confidential helpline, training seminars for healthcare and other professionals, and an online shop, which sells, among other items, literature, bedwetting alarms, daytime pants and bedding protection.

Recent campaigns ERIC has run include *The Right to Go*, to highlight every child's right to good care for a continence problem at school and access to safe and hygienic school toilets at all times, and *Let's Talk About Poo*, to raise awareness of children's poo problems.

ERIC's website (www.eric.org.uk) is packed with information on all aspects of children's toileting, including soiling problems. There is also a website to encourage healthy bowels in children, which includes the Let's Talk About Poo Game: letstalkaboutpoo.eric.org.uk

You can contact ERIC in the following ways:

Telephone:
Helpline and information:
   0845 370 8008 (within the UK only)
   Telephone charges apply, please check website for current rates.
Main switchboard:
   0117 960 3060 (within the UK)
   +44 117 960 3060 (from outside the UK)

Postal address:
ERIC
36 Old School House
Britannia Road
Kingswood
BRISTOL
BS15 8DB
United Kingdom

ERIC is a small charity working in an unglamorous area and reliant on donations. Please consider donating money or fundraising for ERIC so that it can continue its vital work for children and families. ERIC receives all profits from sales of the author's books which are sold through their online shop.

ERIC is a Registered Charity (no 1002424) and a Company Limited by Guarantee (no 2580579) registered in England and Wales.